or else the light

Izzy John

BookLeaf Publishing

Presentation by *BookLeaf Publishing*

Web: www.bookleafpub.com

E-mail: info@bookleafpub.com

ISBN: 9789357447447

First edition 2021

DEDICATION

According to the blog 'Counting Dead Women', in the 28 weeks following the murder of Sarah Everard, 81 more women were allegedly killed by men in the UK. This collection is dedicated to their memories, and their names.

Sarah Everard, Geetika Goyal, Imogen Bohajczuk, Wenjing Xu, Karen McClean, Stacey Knell, Smita Mistry, Sammy Mills, Patricia Audsley, Phyllis Nelson, Klaudia Soltys, Simone Ambler, Emma McArthur, Sherrie Milnes, Constanta Bune, Jacqueline Grant, Loretta Herman, Egle Vengaliene, Sally Metcalf, Sarah Keith, Peggy Wright, Charmaine O'Donnell, Michelle Cooper, Kerry Bradford, Julia James, Beth Aspey, Susan Booth, Mayra Zulfiqar, Maria Rawlings, Chenise Gregory, Agnes Akom, Wendy Cole, Caroline Crouch, Svetlana Mihalachi, Nicola Kirk, Unnamed woman, Agita Geslere, Lauren Wilson, Peninah Kabeba, Jill Hickery, Bethany Vincent, Esther Brown, Michaela Hall, Mildred Whitmore, Stacey Clay, Linda Hood, Marlene Coleman, Sophie Cartlidge, Gracie Spinks, Michelle Hibbert, Kim Dearden, Sally Poynton,

Catherine Wardleworth, Sukhjit Badial, Elsie Pinder, Catherine Stewart, Ishrat Ahmed, Tamara Padi, Katie Brankin, Sandra Hughes, Beatrice Stoica, Pat Holland, Yordanos Brhane, Amanda Selby, Louise Kam, Malgorzata Lechanska, Megan Newborough, Diana Nichols, Maxine Davison, Kate Shepherd, Bella Nicandro, Eileen Barrott, Sharon Pickles, Helen Anderson, Jade Ward, Maddie Durdant-Hollamby, Fawziyah Javed, Ingrid Matthew, Sabina Nessa, Unnamed woman, Terri Harris, Sukhjeet Uppal.

ACKNOWLEDGEMENT

This collection would not have been possible without my fantastic English teachers in secondary school - Mrs Day, Mrs Addison and Mr Forbes - who all fostered a life-long love for poetry in me. It is a privilege to now work every day to do the same for my own students, who continuously inspire me with their curiosity and ideas.

An incalculable amount of gratitude is owed to my friends 'The Thursgay gang'. Without their irreverence and hilarity, I would not have the emotional capacity to think about - and come back from - the dark stuff of life. They truly are both ship and anchor to me, and Soph, my partner, is my harbour in every storm. Thank you for being.

My life has been made richer by the exceptional work of many artists, but the verbal virtuosity of some in particular have warmed my blood on the worst of days - the musicians Tori Amos and Grace Petrie, the poets Andrea Gibson and Carol Ann Duffy, the writers Jeanette Winterson and Margaret Atwood. The last line of Atwood's seminal work, 'The Handmaid's Tale', forms the title of this collection, echoing the light that I hope seeps through the pages. Thank you for singing/writing me and countless others through countless things.

Finally, thanks to anyone anywhere who carries on the fight against VAWG, political injustice, social inequality, poverty and the forces that fight to make a lesser world. Whether you are a volunteer, a donor, a worker, an artist, an activist or anything else - your work is life saving and life changing. Hold on to that when it all feels too much.

PREFACE

It is hard to pinpoint the exact time when poetry moved into my life with significant force. Poetry was always in my mother's mouth and to this day we sometimes recite as we walk together - although her memory is far superior to mine. As a teenager I wrote voraciously and naturally a large amount of it was cliched, emotional and trying to be the writer I wanted to be, or thought I should be. Nonetheless the transformative power I felt with a pen in my hand endured, and occasionally now, I come across scraps of paper from my adolescent years and can see the roots of my - hopefully more authentic voice - sprouting tentatively on post-it notes and diary entries.

Some of the poems that are present in this book had their first iteration during a hugely formative module during my university years. Dubbed 'Reeling and Writhing', a small group of us were tasked with exploring established narratives - myths, bible stories, fables and legends - and then re-writing, re-centring or re-imagining them in our own voices. More than a decade on, I find myself teaching my A-level students 'The World's Wife', by Carol Ann Duffy, and feeling its resonance in a way that feels both prophetic and present. I could not but help weaving the myths which have fascinated me for so long in amongst this collection. Shakespeare's characters and words crop up too, occasionally - an inevitable cliché, perhaps, coming from an English teacher, but honestly one that felt as natural to me as telling my own stories.

Looking back, the threads that have always been present in my own work are women and nature - both of which have astonishing capacity for beauty, rage, growth, power and hope against all the odds. Nature, then, is a key element which I used to frame my collection. As with many others, the experience of lockdown sharpened my focus on the small, alive things in the world - flower petals, bees, the loveliness of a twisted tree branch. In amongst the loss and howling storms of womanhood, things bloom. I wanted and needed to be reminded of that, in my own words.

Most importantly, this collection deliberately looks to and comments on the present as well as the myths of the past. I committed to its publication in the week that the murderer of Sarah Everard was placed on trial. The weight of that awful event, and the concurrent murder of

Sabina Nessa, became the gravity holding this collection together in a way that I could not have anticipated. My words are poor in comparison to what needs to be said, but I hope that they articulate even a fraction of the rage and grief felt by many, collectively, on those terrible days. As long as patriarchal power structures - be they personal, social, cultural or political - are used to suppress and coerce, oppress and mock, torture and kill, I will do my best to dismantle them. As long as women and girls are victims of that violence, I will strive to use my voice to fight for them.

Ophelia

drowning sent me down
into dark, brackish waters. I
emerged clean, baptised, surrounded
by women and girls, doing laundry and
laughing on the banks of the Styx.

In life we were quiet, demure, compliant -
death shattered the locks on our voices
the box of our secrets split and spilled,
overflowing into this dark hall. Here
the walls ring with chatter, banter, patois,
giggles, cusses, offers of tea and gin,
Persephone's pomegranates pass from
hand to hand. Here there is song and fire
at our hearth. We sit in state,
history's matriarchs: from fairy tales,
myth, the East End, palaces, parliaments,
prisons, Salem, street corners.
We take it in turns
to tell our tales, pass cigarettes
and stories round. 'My turn', says Diana,
Cinders, Sylvia, Benazir, Galatea, Anne B
(and the rest). We gather to
break our silence and bread,
set food and truth at the feet of the dead.

With every soul sent here in blood
we swell our ranks. We bide
our time. We send our signals
to the other side of
the river - where violets grow in
pavement cracks, where DNA
tells tales, where courage lifts
its head against the odds.
Where trees burst through concrete walls,
where storms raise hell
and soil renews
and refuge is found
and songs are sung
where our myths become matter, magic
under mother's tongues
where our names are spoken
like a refrain. Where women
and girls pulled out of water
float up
again.

We float again, alive
in this dark hall. Our voices
are jellyfish with the strength to drown.
We rise like dust. Adieu, Hamlet.

Remember us.

sunset

Roxanne checks the last tube home
Maria texts her sister the time
Becky moves her keys to her hand
Eloise stays for another half

Zoe goes over defensive moves
Busaad takes the well lit path
Lara checks the Uber driver reviews
Maria texts her mum just in case

Kav gets a mate to walk her back
Umaira covers her headscarf up
Lizzie changes her outfit again
Roxanne leaves before the sun goes down

Lara gets the bus instead
Sabina puts her headphones on
Jessie turns on "what three words"
Flo decides to stay at home

Amie shifts her pepper spray
Eloise stays til closing time
Lizzie switches her skirt for jeans
Amina snaps her gum on the tube

Ilana takes the short cut home
Imogen goes the long way round
Sophie's mum waits by the door
Sabina takes her headphones off

Sam has her hand on her rape alarm
Nic and Lexi don't hold hands
Harriet puts her hoodie up
Safiyah keeps her eyes ahead

Busaad crosses the road again
Jessie makes a fake phone call
Amina gets off two stops early
Ros double knots her trainer lace

Sabina tries to memorize his face.

Becky's keys turn in the lock
Lara's bus is running late
Ilana jogs the last hundred steps
Sophie's mum waits by the door

Sophie gets in just after one
Harriet puts her hoodie down
Charlie avoids the lads in the park
Jessie releases her pent up breath

Kav texts her mate to say thanks again
Eloise can't remember his name

Roxanne gets cat called in the gym
Annie orders more pepper spray.

We're different women in daylight,
but in darkness, the same.

glass bricks

In the early morning glow
of my commuter train, mid-way
through the summer term, I think
how no one ever told me what teaching
is. It is weathering the waves of
a hundred heartless headlines
decrying our laziness, audacity, lack of capacity.
Holidaymakers. Soft bastards.
Union scum. I have to imagine myself a cliff
eroded from underneath - but still
outlasting the words from people
who have never set foot in a classroom.
I have to remind myself that they
have never known what it is to prise a mind
open, like an oyster, thumb its pearl to a shine.
I know what it is
to hold a world in four walls
and thirty two desks. I know
what it is to be lifeboat and water and
lighthouse.
I've know what is to build myself
out of glass bricks,
to show how to make a life.

And they will never know how

every day is a kaleidoscope,
a roller coaster,
a battlefield, a therapist's sofa,
a comedian's stage, a theatre for the brave,
a pilgrimage, a paint-by-numbers.
They'll never know
how many friendships I've helped
patch together, the storms and seasons
I weather in the span of a day.
How many names I've memorised -
a hymn that echo in my mind, years down the
line.

How I still wonder, after all this time,
if the lessons I taught helped
shape a life in any small way. How
some kids' faces never leave you.
How you become new-born
when you put that 'Sir' or 'Miss'
in front of your own name
and have to learn yourself all over again.

And I would tell them that I am a cliff,
stubborn against the waves.
Subject to attrition, yes,
but full of strength, and stalwart nonetheless.

hands

I never knew palm prints
could burn without scarring.
I never knew fingers could
steal without warning. I know
now what hands can do, the pinch
of finger and thumb,
the turning of skin into prison,
of flesh into memory. How touch
becomes flinch and caress becomes
risk. A kiss to a fist in the
blink of an eye.

I am careful, now, with
my own hands. I hold my
palms out and up. I think
of what my friend told me
years ago, how seven years
will see your whole skin shed,
regrown, renewed. You have
no hold on me now.

five moments of doubt / Eurydice

I couldn't help but think
What-might-have-been, even years later.

If when he had seen that crack of light
parting the earth like hopeful lips
he had heeded that strange force, simply
Looked Back
and exploded me into ash.

I suppose
we were happy at first,
falling-in-love-again. The sex was thrilling,
but I couldn't help but see
how his eyes slid up and down
those tender green-shooted boys
who came by for singing lessons.

And when we settled
into distanced ways -
polite greetings, pass-the-jam
I-have-to-work-late-again -

that strange mixture of
pain and relief -

and grief, for the girl who believed in
the love-of-my-life, who
believed in the songs, the ballads,
the lyrics, the rhymes, the key
changes, the sea changes, the
time after times - and settled
for this, for the safety of
something. for the girl who
believed he was better than
nothing.

And when we fought
over fighting
and slammed the door
and stormed out
and came back
and made up
It was good to remember
that I tasted like dirt.

And then we gave up
and feigned sleep
night after night,
our breaths even and slow.
And when we went cold
and silent as snow, grew

old together/apart -
I thought of that light
crowbarring the earth open. How
his damn indecision ruined
that one chance we had to be happy.

prayers of the agnostic

the more I think about god -
whatever they are - the more
I think that they must take form
in tomatoes. Think of the yearly glut.
The way nature spills her guts for us
every summer, how she grows green
into red, splits the sides of
fragrant globes too ripe
for containment. Some people find
god in unfortunate events, in luck,
in the grace of reprieve, in church,
in chance. for me the vine
heavy under my palms, giving,
grafting through frost, gifting
the fruit - for sauce, sandwiches,
a neighbour offering spares. For being
popped like a glowing sweet
right then and there,
the warmth of seeds on my tongue like a prayer.

role playing

be a good girl. don't answer back.
what if he's mean? then answer back.
you answered back? well what did you
expect. next time tell someone.
you told someone? well they won't like that.
try talking it out. use your words.
did you use your words? well why did you
swear?
no wonder he got angry. you're better
than that. just avoid him. did you
avoid him? well he's probably hurt,
boys have feelings too you know. you should
show
more kindness. did you ask him to play?
and he touched you where? well were the rules
of the
game absolutely clear? well it's just this one
time, I'm sure of that. he did it again? well
he probably likes you
just give it some time, set him the example.
what did he call you? well, sticks and stones.
where did he touch you?
what word did he use? well growing up is
hard. what did he want? well boys will be
boys. be a good girl. be kind. be inclusive.

rise above it, don't answer back, use your words
report it, don't report it, avoid him,
include him, cover up, be proud of your
body, tell someone, don't snitch. Boys
become men. Show him what that means.

Nightwalking

I carve my fist into a mouth with metal teeth

I become owl like, my head twisting and
rotating from side to side
at unnatural angles.
I wish I had the power of that panoramic
predator
to see in the dark
to see the flicker of a mouse
the vibration of a van door or the
shift in the step of a stranger.
I try not to think of myself as vulnerable
Whilst hovering over the dial button
Three digits under my thumb
Useless bullets in a useless gun
I weigh my bag to feel its potential as weapon.
I hold my breath like a birthday balloon
not daring to let it go until under the safety of a
roof.

A mnemonic floats to the front of my mind -
S I N G solar plexus instep nose groin -
I panic when I can't remember what the solar
plexus is

I panic when I remember I've never thrown a
punch
I panic when I remember people will ask what
was she wearing.
I pull up my hood, pull down my coat,
try to be invisible whilst
seeking out street lights
pools of safety
lily pads in dark water.
I lift my face to every corner where cameras
may lurk.

We all do the dance -
the crossing the road,
the doubling back,
the lifting of our chins in false bravery.
The deliberate, careful, staying behind of any
men we see.
The deliberate, careful, calculation of how far
that one is behind me.
The deliberate, careful, mapping of the route -
the nearest shop,
the short cuts to avoid.
We keep our pace measured.
We try to not think of the word "target" or
the statistics,
or the stories we know.
We think about the last person who spoke to us.
Will they remember to check if we got home?

We think about if we will get home.

Sarah Everard
is every one of us -
was every one of us.

Every one of us could have been her, on that
street, under those cameras.
Snatched from that dark water
her balloon of breath bursting
                    the dance ending,
                            the teeth of her fist closing on
nothing but air.

PTSD

It sometimes hits out of nowhere:
a moment of freezing. Not
freezing like ice or like
winter's mornings -
but freezing like statue,
petrified by gorgon.

It comes out of nowhere
these moments of pausing.
Sometimes out of a headline
that pops up whilst scrolling,
sometimes out of a touch
that comes without warning.
Sometimes out of a daydream,
that sensation of falling.

But sometimes
there's a second
where susurrus stirs me.
Sometimes there's a minute
where inertia starts melting.

I live for those moments
of sharp fizzing lightning -

lemonade bright in my bones
bubbling, lightening.

I, Caliban

ten years and eight months
and my mother hands me
a hand-held mirror, tells me
to have a look between my legs.
How simple it was. The pleasure
of the word on my tongue, teeth
pressed to my lips forming a v - I
loved words, even then, the way
the world glowed with these
new-to-me sounds.

But that was back then.

Now I look at myself and
my whorls of flesh, velvet depths.
I feel my mother's voice drowning
in euphemisms, insults, filth,
labiaplasty, FGM, abuse, shame -
the strange, awful power of a name.

Perhaps there are things
that shouldn't be named.
I am stripped raw by syllables
I am incandescent with rage
that such an innocent thing

be twisted into language. The
red plague rid you.

escalator

you turn to me, stark against store lights,
as if to ask a question, or to point out a butterfly.
When the ninth step becomes the tenth, you
bend down
and kiss me. Your mouth burns on mine,
the point of a struck match. It tastes
like brown sugar.

when we step
off onto solid ground
the solidity of not rising
up makes me ache.

when people ask later
when I knew that I loved you
it is that moment between ninth and tenth
becoming
that remains.

prayers of the agnostic

please let it rain tomorrow
please let him ask me
dear God, I know we've not
talked in a while - but could
you do this one thing, if you're
there and not too busy?
please tell me what to do
please keep them safe.
please stop the war.
please tell me I didn't leave my keys in the door.
please let me win
please let them lose
please give me a raise
please get me out
please let me go
please give me a sign
please let that not be my boss
on the phone. please let me make
the last train home. please give
all the deserving ones a chance.
please unsend that email. please
let me get home safe. please

give us a child. please give us
more time. Dear god I know
I've not been faithful or sure
or kept in touch, but I swear if you
do this one thing I'll come
back to church, praise your name,
sing hymns, do whatever. just please this one
thing Lord, amen now and forever.

insomnia

A single kiss changed her world:
thorns withered, walls fell.
The dawn unfolded like a fist,
fairies fled like light in winter.

She waited what seemed
like a century
for her wedding night,
but not long enough to have dreamt
how flat and hard
his hand would be
against her cheek.
When she slept, she'd wake up
screaming, dreaming
of spindles, and his lukewarm lips.

Over the years, she fades,
doesn't speak, grows thin as gruel.
Watches the ceiling for days on
end. Cyanotic madness fills
her skull. Sometimes she scrapes
the skin from her mouth
as if she could scald off
the memory of what she
can't remember. She

doesn't know if she wants
to remember.

The doctors visit the attic
clinking chains of polysyllables
meant to cure: lorazepam,
trazodone, complex trauma
disorder, agoraphobia,
dissociation, hypnotherapy -
flashback, psychotic
break, dyssomnia. All in
your head, my dear.
Try lavender oil, herbal tea.
Try to stick to a routine.
Fresh air will do you
the world of good.

The wallpaper in the room
fades to yellow. Mutates, balloons
into mushrooming wraiths. She waits,
cringes, screams, hallucinates -
no one believes her, no one ever
believed her. Shapes shift in the
silken walls, and sleep never comes.

what was he wearing?

a suit and tie - pale blue shirt
a Grateful Dead tee
flannel pyjamas
a condom
a hoodie, faded
Christmas socks
a mask
jeans and high tops
police uniform
something green and itchy
designer underwear
shitty underwear
a Rolex
a fitbit
a festival wristband
shorts, cuffed, denim
the sweater I gave him last birthday
his Man U strip
nothing
school jumper and a beanie
a kind expression
nothing that stood out, you know

nothing that said he would
take without asking.

osteogenesis / Galatea

When I came to life
I was scarred across the belly and back -
He hadn't thought that being split out of ivory
crack by crack would hurt. I felt like an egg
with its insides scooped out.

Still shell-like, the sun shone through my
porcelain skin,
silhouetting the lovely arrogance of sculpted
limbs.
Pygmalion always had a weakness for pretty
things
and was in such a rush to fuck me that
he broke one of my ribs - it tore through me with
shivers
that he mistook for orgasm. Hah! My spat-out
words
were less delicate, smashing plates, hating his
sex,
roughened by tequila and cigarettes.
I drank and smoked to warm myself, because he
couldn't.

Sometimes he would just sit and look
at me. I imagined the art critics:
“The lines are there, but the whole thing is lost
in negative space”. Just as much a book as a
body,
my spine worn with overturning and turning
over:
well-thumbed, torn, stained and bound.
Pygmalion did not me her read, he said it would
ruin my eyesight. I was good for other things:
I gave birth to a son, pebble-freckled,
brittle-boned, who became an island.

COP26

Persephone spends her days
chained to the wheels of planes,
blockading motorways, sticking it
to the man, boss, king, god -
all of the above. The group chat
goes nuts on the live stream:
Nadia Nazar, Greta T,
Juwari Jama, Artemisa Xakriabá -
the crew, the new green deal,
the youth, Gen Z, the movers
and shakers, the hell raisers,
the best of us,
and the last fucking chance
we can afford.

life sentence / 30.9.21

a life sentence, in spite of its weight
feels horribly light: maybe the
bible was right on this one - a eye
for a eye - but then it's not a life for a life
- it's the rest of his life for all of her lives,
plus all of the lives of those who are left,
bereft of her thousand futures, her
chances, dances, moments and years -
no, a life sentence is horribly light.

We all think the same, in our guts and our brains
-
justice is served but revenge feels more right.
We want horrible darkness, not getting off
lightly. And a life sentence is light when it's
weighed against women: our safety,
our lives. A life sentence is nothing when
she's not alive.

If I had the might of my ancestor witches...you
know,
I'm not sure that I'd care what was 'right'.

I'm pretty sure after all that he's done
I'd take an eye for an eye, and a life for a life.

marigolds

All of the baking summer season
I watched the marigolds grow in
my neighbour's window boxes: blush then
bloom with brash orange, brazen scarlet,
eking out the warmth of those sultry days.

despite the thunderstorms, fractious
at the turning of autumn
they still remained - yes, a little
worse for wear, but marigolds
nonetheless.

Dying suns at the end of
a world. Solstice passes, and it's only
eight days of steady rain that
collapses them, imploding stars
into shredded silk, bare stems.
I note their passing with strange, calm
joy; I scribble it down: 'isn't it good
to be reminded that not all decay is ugly,
that not all change needs to be feared?'
My therapist says I'm making progress,
reminds me that slow and steady
wins the race. The patient, empty soil
is vibrant with promise. It is enough to wait.

mushrooms and garlic

There is such comfort in the
countless normal moments.
When I am sick, my girlfriend
cooks me mushrooms even though
she hates mushrooms. She
steams them in their own breath, adds garlic,
turns it to gold, fills the whole house with
healing spells. We all hold Midas' magic,
most days, in our own ways. May we be
less wanton than he, foolish King,
who forgot that a buttercup
in sunlight will bear us treasure. My love
brings me bread. We eat together.
May we always see and seek
the good in each other.

liminal space

the train home from school at
the end of the term
steamy with rain. Solstice a half-
faded memory, and evening's dark
thickening. Despite this, today
is a good day to be less afraid -
to be brave, even. To think of how
when we have our children
we can teach them
to make the leek babka I love,
to learn the names of flowers,
to listen to the stories of women
who need to be heard. To live
a whole, apple-bright, gleaming life.

I step off the train, lift my chin
to the sky.
My heart floats out of my chest
like a weightless kite.

www.ingramcontent.com/pod-product-compliance
Lightning Source LLC
Chambersburg PA
CBHW051742130826
49812CB00033B/969

* 9 7 8 9 3 5 7 4 4 7 4 4 7 *